Y0-DNM-738

LGBTQ+: Acronym for Lesbian, Gay, Bisexual, Transgender and Queer

Queer: People use this word as a way to identify with and celebrate people of all gender identities and all the ways people love each other. When used in a mean way, it is a word that hurts.

-Human Rights Campaign

*This is the LGBTQ+ community's current flag. Because the community is always changing, so is it's flag. This Flag is important because it represents the different qualities of the community and is a symbol of **pride!***

Hi! My name is Emily. I am from Boston, Massachusetts. Boston is a cool place to live because we have a lot of people who work hard everyday to make Boston a more inclusive and welcoming place.

Today I want to introduce you to some of the people who worked to make Boston a safe and happy place for people in the LGBTQ+ community!

The first person I want to introduce you to is **Thomas Morton**. Thomas was a Pilgrim who left Plymouth Plantation in 1622 because he did not like their strict rules. He started his own colony called **Merrymount**, where Quincy, MA stands today.

Fun Fact: Because the people of Merrymount where no longer forced to follow Puritan religion, a lot of them worshipped Greek Gods. They would even have community celebrations to honor these Gods.

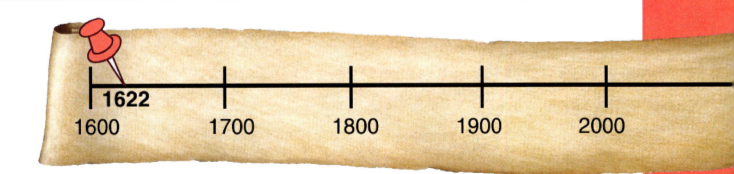

1622
1600   1700   1800   1900   2000

Many pilgrims left with Thomas, including those who were LGBTQ+ because they could date whoever they loved in Merrymount. Thomas' bravery in doing what he thought was right helped give LGBTQ+ Bostonians a home.

Unfortunately, in the past few Massachusetts communities were as welcoming to LGBTQ+ people as Merrymount was. Most towns and cities had strict rules about how they expected people to act and behave. For example, girls used to only be allowed to wear dresses and boys were only allowed to wear pants. But some individuals thought these rules were unfair and fought against them.

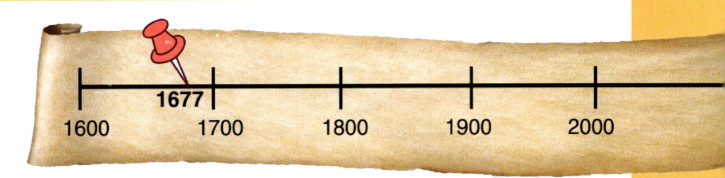

1677

1600   1700   1800   1900   2000

Meet **Dorothie Hoyt**. Dorothie was arrested in Salisbury in 1677 for wearing pants that were viewed as too boyish. Her punishment included being thrown in jail until her father could pay the court 40 shillings worth of money or corn. Even after being arrested, Dorothie continued to wear boyish clothes because she liked them!

Another pair of women who fought against these rules were **Annie Fields** and **Sarah Jewett**. In the 1880s two women were not allowed to legally marry each other, but Annie and Sarah where so in love that they decided to have a secret marriage ceremony. They spent their days writing each other love poems and traveling together.

In the late 1800s there were other Massachusetts' women like Annie and Sarah who wanted to live together. Two unmarried women living together in Massachusetts soon gained popularity and became known as a **Boston Marriage**.

1600   1700   1800   **1880**   1900   2000

Beloved, when I see thee sleeping there,
And watch the tender curving of thy mouth,
The cheek, our home of kisses, the soft hair,
And over all a languor of the south;
And marked thy house of thought, thy forehead, where
All trouble of the earth was then at rest,
And thy dear eyes, a blessing to the blest,
Their ivory gates closed on this world of care—
—Annie Fields

Please put your hands together for **Sylvia Sidney**! Sylvia is one of Boston's most famous drag queens. **Drag** is a creative performance used to express one's feelings about gender and gender rules. Drag shows have always been important for the LGBTQ+ community because they are a safe space, where LGBTQ+ people can express themselves without judgement or fear.

When Sylvia first started performing Drag in 1940, he was not well liked. At his first drag show he was booed off the stage. After a pep talk from the pianist, who found him crying backstage, Sylvia went back on stage and performed his routine. He went on to become an inspiration to many other Boston queens.

1600   1700   1800   1900   **1940**   2000

Fun Fact: Up until the 1960s Boston held an annual Beaux Drag Ball known for the extravagant costumes of its performers. Hundreds of people from across the country would travel to Boston each year to see these Balls!

Fun Fact: Drag became popular in Boston in the 1940s after clubs like Jacques Cabaret and Playland opened. Jacques Cabaret was Boston's longest running LGBTQ+ establishment.

12

Drag shows and other **LGBTQ+ safe spaces** allowed the community to grow. Soon the LGBTQ+ community and its allies, people who supported them, had a bigger voice and began coordinating efforts to increase equality.

In 1971 Boston's LGBTQ+ community decided to march to demand that Boston provide them with equal access to jobs, housing, and health care, as well as for the right to hold hands or kiss in public without being arrested.

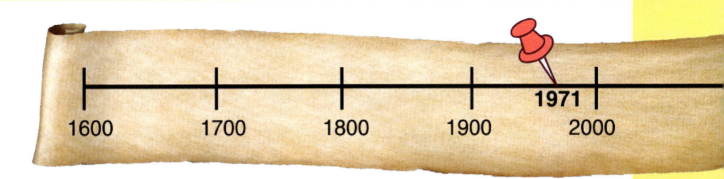

1971

1600   1700   1800   1900   2000

At this march, Boston's LGBTQ+ community invited **Reverend Goddess Megora Kennedy**, a well-known Black, LGBTQ+ activist, to read off a list of demands. She was asked, in part, because she participated in **Stonewall**, the New York LGBTQ+ protest that inspired this **Boston march**.

Fun Fact:
To honor Stonewall and other LGBTQ+ marches, June is recognized as Pride Month, which is often celebrated with parades throughout the country.

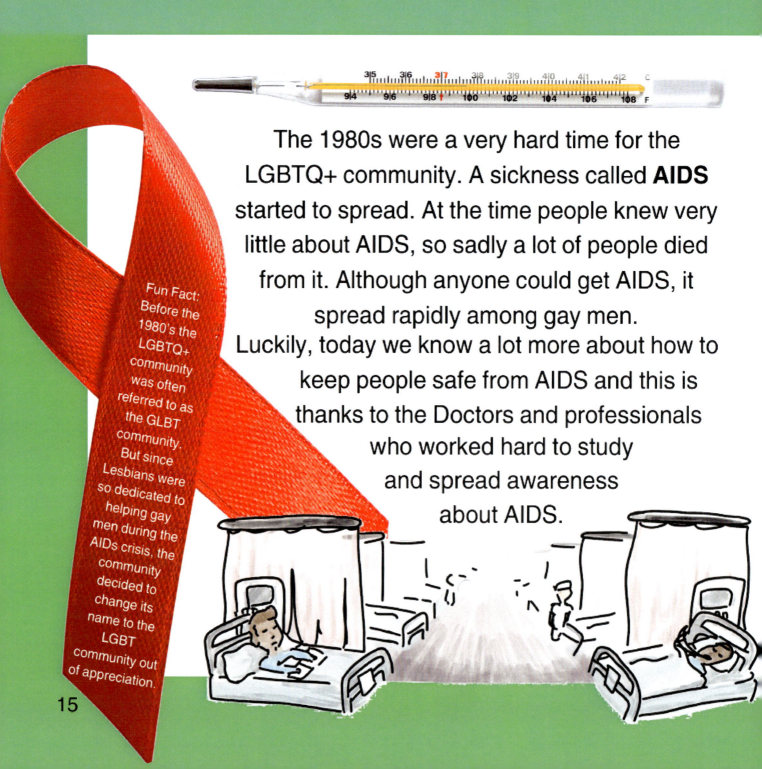

The 1980s were a very hard time for the LGBTQ+ community. A sickness called **AIDS** started to spread. At the time people knew very little about AIDS, so sadly a lot of people died from it. Although anyone could get AIDS, it spread rapidly among gay men.

Luckily, today we know a lot more about how to keep people safe from AIDS and this is thanks to the Doctors and professionals who worked hard to study and spread awareness about AIDS.

Fun Fact: Before the 1980's the LGBTQ+ community was often referred to as the GLBT community. But since Lesbians were so dedicated to helping gay men during the AIDs crisis, the community decided to change its name to the LGBT community out of appreciation.

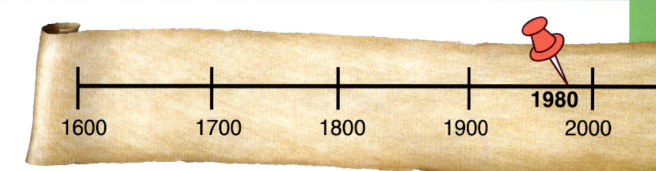

1600　　　1700　　　1800　　　1900　　**1980**　2000

Meet **Dr. Kenneth Mayer**, he was one of these doctors. He worked for **Fenway Health**, a healthcare center in Boston for LGBTQ+ people. He started Fenway's first AIDS research and community education programs. It was these programs that set Fenway Health apart from other health centers and allowed it to be seen as a leader in AIDS research and education.

Fun Fact: Healthcare centers from across America, and even some abroad, looked to Fenway Health as a blueprint for AIDS research and educational outreach.

The LGBTQ+ community faced even worse discrimination during the AIDS epidemic than they did before. So the community started fighting for legal protections.

Meet **Arline Isaacson**. In 1989 Arline helped advocate for the **Massachusetts' Gay Rights Bill** that would prevent people from being discriminated against because of who they loved. This allowed women who loved other women and men who loved other men to be open about their love without fear of being fired from their job or denied housing. This bill went on to inspire other LGBTQ+ bills like **Freedom for all Massachusetts** in 2018, which prevented discrimination against anyone in the LGBTQ+ community.

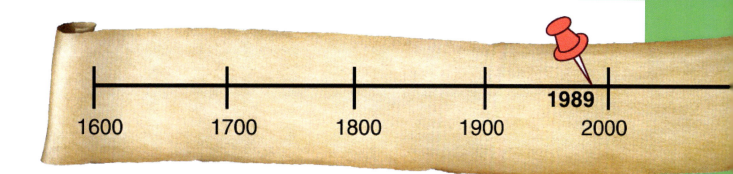

1600　　　1700　　　1800　　　1900　**1989**　2000

Fun Fact:
The Freedom law received support from the Patriots, Red Sox, Bruins, New England Revolution, and Celtics. Every New England professional sports team publicly endorsed this law.

I Voted

Arline Isaacson

Even though the LGBTQ+ community now had legal protections against discrimination, they still did not have all the same rights as non-LGBTQ+ people. For example, a Massachusetts law only allowed a child to have one legal mom and one legal dad. This narrow definition of family made it extra hard for LGBTQ+ couples to have legal rights as parents. But thanks to two Boston surgeons, this law changed.

Meet **Dr. Susan Love** and her long-term partner **Dr. Helen Cooksey**. Together they raised a daughter named **Tammy**. In 1993 they fought for the right to both be Tammy's legal mothers and won! This lawsuit opened the door for other same-sex couples to be recognized for their rights as parents in Massachusetts.

1600   1700   1800   1900   **1993** 2000

Slowly, the LGBTQ+ community started to gain representation in leadership. Meet **Kenneth Reeves** who was elected mayor of Cambridge in 1992. Kenneth faced a lot of hate while running for mayor because he was Black and gay, but by persisting anyway he made history. He was the first Black, gay mayor in the entire United States!

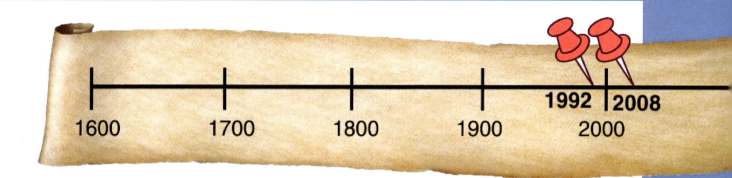

1600 1700 1800 1900 **1992** 2000 **2008**

The great thing about people standing up for themselves and their community is that it inspires and opens the door for others to do the same. In 2008 **Denise Simmons** ran and was elected mayor of Cambridge. She too made history as Massachusetts' first Black female mayor and the United State's first Black, lesbian mayor!

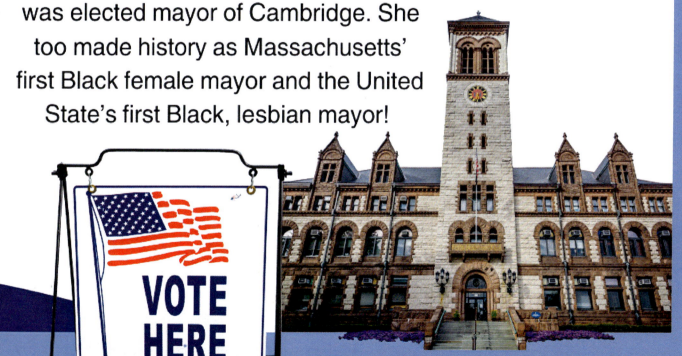

22

On May 17, 2004, Massachusetts made history again by becoming the first state to allow same-sex marriage. **Marcia Kadish** and **Tanya McCloskey** got married in Cambridge City Hall and were the first same-sex couple to legally marry in the United States!

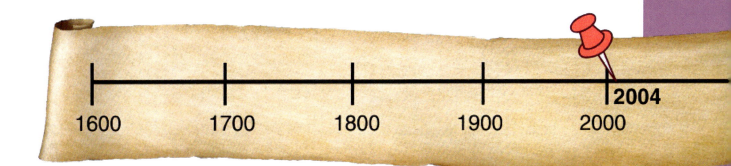

1600   1700   1800   1900   **2004**   2000

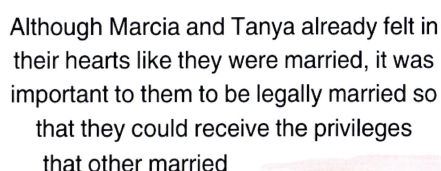

Although Marcia and Tanya already felt in their hearts like they were married, it was important to them to be legally married so that they could receive the privileges that other married partners received, like health care, financial, and legal benefits.

Fun Fact: Marcia and Tanya did not plan to make history as the first same-sex marriage. They only arrived to the court house early so they could spend the whole day celebrating with other couples who could finally get married!

24

Lastly, let me introduce you to **Ashton Mota**. Ashton is a young activist from Lowell! Since he was 14, Ashton has been advocating for LGBTQ+ youth. Specifically people's right to define their gender however feels best for them. He also advocates for them to be able to use the restrooms and play on the sports teams that match that gender identity.

President Joe Biden

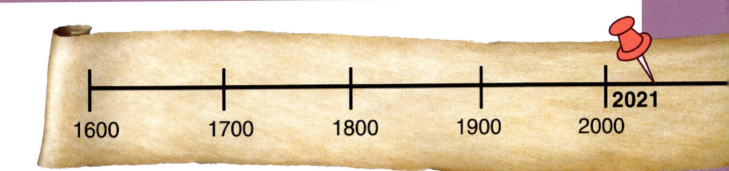

2021

1600   1700   1800   1900   2000

In 2021, when Ashton was 16, he was invited to speak at the White House's Pride celebration, at which he advocated for the **Equality Act**. A law that would protect this right for people in all states!

Boston's LGBTQ History ✓
@BostonsLGBTQHistory

"It's simple. When children are loved, we thrive." -Ashton Mota
#Go_Vote

25 June 2021

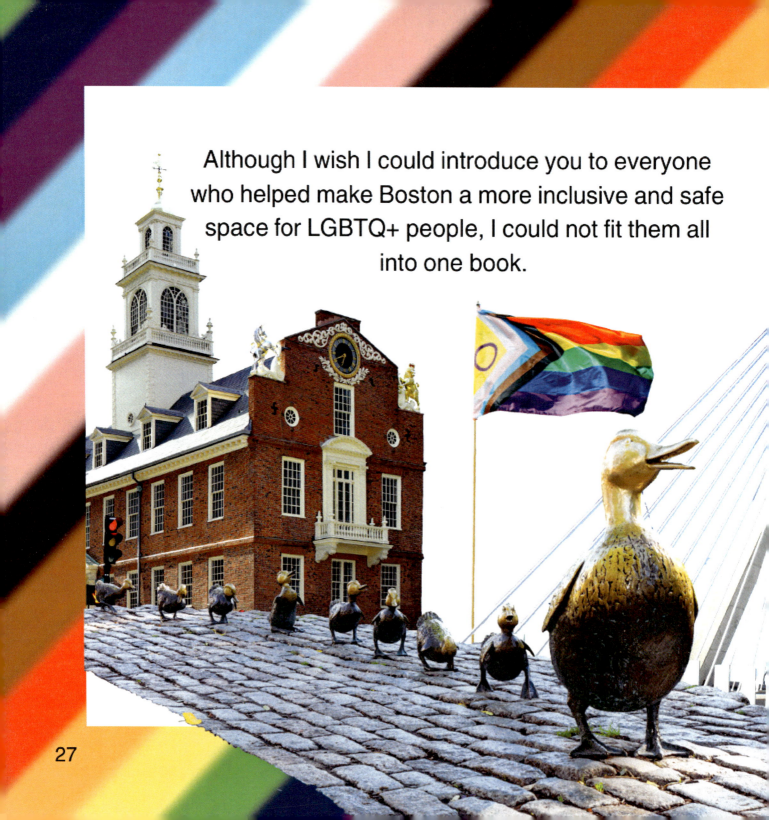

Although I wish I could introduce you to everyone who helped make Boston a more inclusive and safe space for LGBTQ+ people, I could not fit them all into one book.

27

Every LGBTQ+ person and their allies to ever live in Boston and live their life their way is an LGBTQ+ activist and has helped create the Boston we know today! My hope is each of us continues to work towards making our own communities safe spaces for everyone.

Change
Just Ahead

From the Author

Thank you so much for reading my book! I believe that LGBTQ+ history is everyone's history and I am happy to be able to share with you a side of Boston's history which is often ignored. I am so grateful for all the wonderful people who believed in me and helped me put this book together!

As a disclaimer I want to mention that Boston's LGBTQ+ history is very diverse and not well recorded. The people included in this book were people who stood out to me and the people whose stories I wanted to tell. This does not mean that they are the only or even the most influential people in Boston's LGBTQ+ history, or that everyone within the LGBTQ+ community has the same opinions on them. I encourage everyone to keep learning about all communities whose histories are often forgotten or misrepresented.

More Resources for Educators and Parents

The History Project

welcomingschools.org

bagly.org

flag.org/resources

glsen.org/elementary-resources

thetrevorproject.org/resources

Made in United States
North Haven, CT
08 June 2023

37525604R00020